First Word Book

This edition produced for Baby's First Book Club®
Bristol, PA 19007

First published in 2000
by Larousse Kingfisher Chambers Inc.

2 4 6 8 10 9 7 5 3

2BFBC/0902/TIMS/SCH/150GPM

LIBRARY OF CONGRESS CATALOGING-IN-PUBLICATION DATA
Stanley, Mandy.
First word book/illustrated by Mandy Stanley.—1st ed.
p. cm.
Summary: An early-vocabulary building book for an adult and a very young child to share.
ISBN 1-58048-234-1
1. Vocabulary—Juvenile literature. [1. Vocabulary.] I. Title. II. Kingfisher first word book.
PE1449.S685 2000
428.1 21—dc21   99-040369

Printed in China

Editor: Camilla Reid
Senior Designer: Sarah Goodwin
Illustrator: Mandy Stanley
Educational consultant: Dr. Jeni Riley

Contents

Suggestions for parents

Sharing a favorite book with your child is an ideal way to help him or her learn to read. This colorful and appealing first word book will be an invaluable aid for looking at, discussing, and labeling everyday objects, and it will help establish the skills needed for confident reading.

Very young children will enjoy browsing through the book, pointing out objects they recognize. Encourage them to tell you what they know about each picture and give them plenty of praise, even if they get things wrong. The book can help toddlers learn about both spoken and written words and the connection between the two. This is important in the early stages of learning to read.

When reading this book with your child, we suggest you follow the steps listed on the next page. Try to create a relaxed atmosphere and allow the child to work at his or her own pace. Above all, remember that in order for learning to be valuable, it should also be fun.

1. Point to the objects on each page. Say the name of each object, then ask the child to repeat it. After several readings, he or she will be able to say the words without prompting.

2. Match the spoken word to the written label next to the picture. Encourage the child to run a finger along the written label (this develops the understanding that a spoken word has a written equivalent).

3. Select a picture label and ask the child to find the same word in the list at the bottom of the page. This teaches the child to recognize the shape of the word, an essential prereading skill. Initially, the child may only realize that the words look the same, but eventually you can point out the shape and distinctive features of the individual letters.

4. Encourage the child to identify words by the initial sound or letter. Then, he or she can figure out that a letter (or group of letters) represents a sound within a word, e.g. the **ch** of chick.

Enjoy your reading!

Jeni Riley

Jeni Riley M.A., Ph.D., Head of Primary Education,
Institute of Education, University of London, England

What is in the bedroom?

teddy bear

ball

pen

pencil

lamp   pen   bed   comb   doll   yo-yo

6

bed

lamp

yo-yo

rug

comb

kite

book

doll

kite   ball   pencil   rug   book   teddy bear

Things we see in the kitchen

fork

knife

spoon

iron

plate

bowl

spoon   mop   bib   jar   mat   pan

jar

mop

bib

pan

mat

cup

cup   fork   bowl   iron   plate   knife

It's time for a bath

bathtub

duck

sponge

towel

toothbrush   sink   potty   door   bathtub   soap

sink

door

mirror

potty

toothpaste

soap

toothbrush

toothpaste   mirror   duck   towel   sponge

Getting dressed

T-shirt

skirt

jeans

sneakers

socks

12

sweater   shoes   cap   T-shirt   skirt   gloves

coat

gloves

sweater

shoes

belt

cap

scarf

sneakers   scarf   belt   jeans   socks   coat

Point to these parts of your body

nose

toe

back

chin

ear   back   nose   hand   knee   foot

ear

hair

foot

arm

hand

eye

leg

knee

hair   eye   arm   leg   chin   toe

What do you like to eat?

bread

pineapple

banana

orange

egg

pie

Popsicle strawberry carrot bread cheese pie

ham

carrot

cheese

apple

strawberry

Popsicle

banana   pineapple   egg   orange   ham   apple

Look around the backyard

butterfly

slug

rake

ant

ladybug

worm spiderweb frog ant gate butterfly

bird

gate

spiderweb

leaf

nest

frog

worm

slug   ladybug   rake   nest   bird   leaf

Let's go to the park

stroller

dog

pond

sandbox

flower   tricycle   skates   seesaw   pond

flower

swing

skates

tricycle

tree

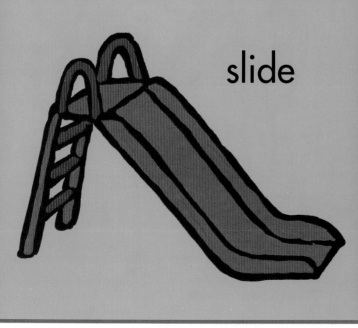

slide

seesaw

swing   tree   sandbox   dog   stroller   slide

There is a lot to do at school

table

teacher

paints

paintbrush

blocks   backpack   blackboard   chair   table

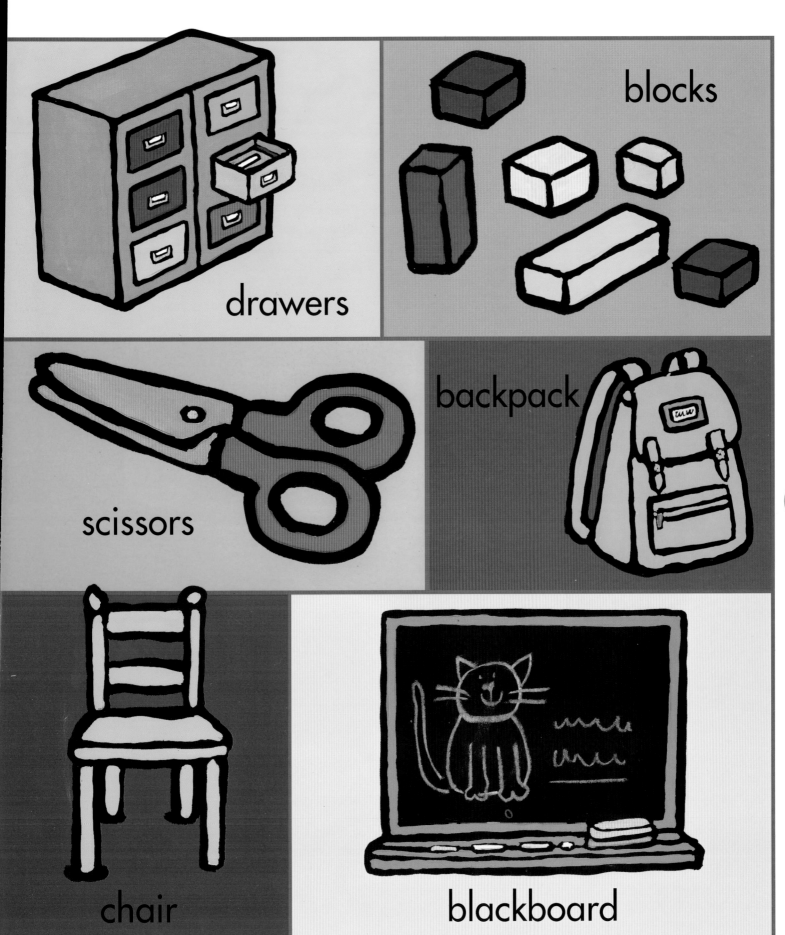

drawers

blocks

scissors

backpack

chair

blackboard

paints   scissors   paintbrush   teacher   drawers

The supermarket is a busy place

milk

jam

cart

clerk

box   purse   can   juice   cash register   money

vegetables

bag

box

can

cash
register

juice

purse

money

vegetables   bag   clerk   milk   cart   jam

We are going to a party

cake

candle

balloon

present

sandwich

noisemaker

bow   candle   candy   hat   present   straw

Jell-O

bow

candy

hat

straw

cake   balloon   sandwich   noisemaker   Jell-O

Who are these people?

man

woman

girl

boy

baby

girl   clown   nurse   boy   dancer   spy

vet

chef

dancer

clown

spy

dentist

nurse

chef   baby   dentist   man   vet   woman

Things that go

ship

rocket

car

airplane

bus

motorcycle　train　bicycle　rocket　truck　car

bicycle

boat

hot-air balloon

truck

motorcycle

train

boat   ship   hot-air balloon   bus   airplane

A day on the farm

tractor

goat

barn

pig

bull

cat   sheep   house   farmer   chick   bull

house

chick

calf

sheep

farmer

cow

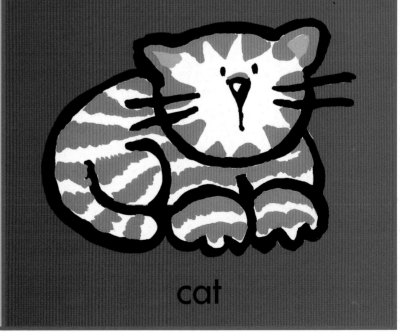

cat

goat   calf   pig   barn   cow   tractor

Where do these animals live?

tiger

wolf

swan

deer

bear   parrot   deer   tiger   seal   monkey

eel

sandcastle

crab

shovel

net

pail

shell

net   shovel   yacht   flip-flops   eel   starfish

What is the weather like?

sun

hail

lightning

fog

rain

storm   wind   ice   hail   cloud   sun

38

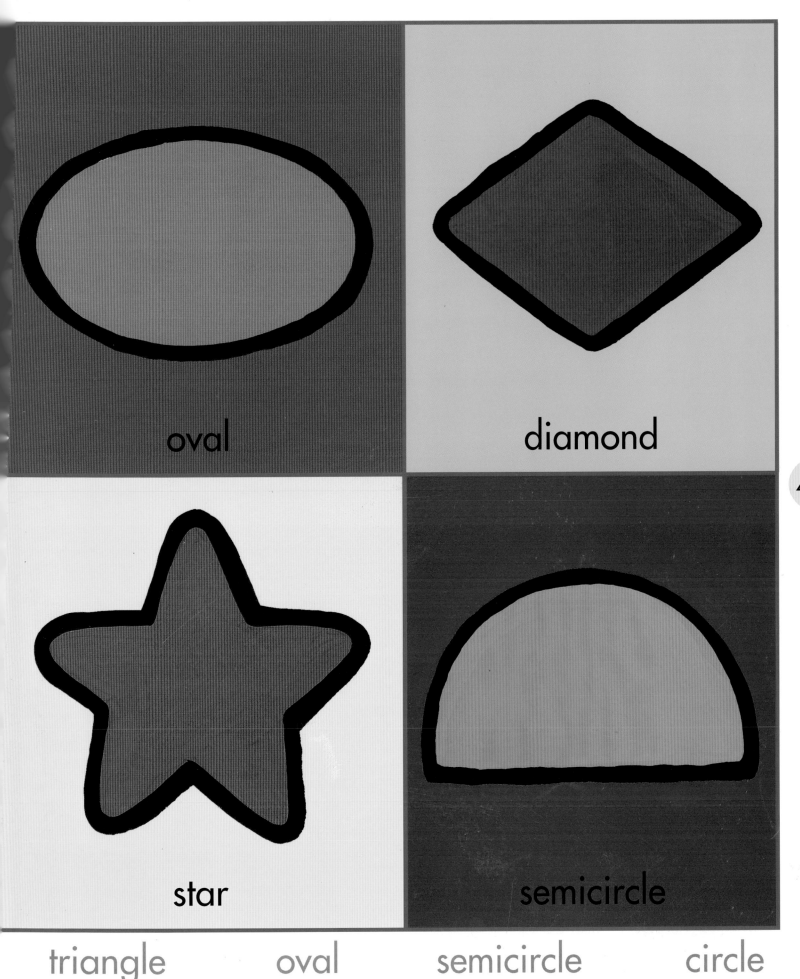

oval

diamond

star

semicircle

triangle   oval   semicircle   circle

All kinds of opposites

fat

thin

old

young

slow

fast

big   young   up   short   fast   thin